How To Use This Study Guide

This five-lesson study guide corresponds to *"The Ministry of the Holy Spirit for the New and Mature Believer" With Rick Renner* (**Renner TV**). Each lesson in this study guide covers a topic that is addressed during the program series, with questions and references supplied to draw you deeper into your own private study of the Scriptures on this subject.

To derive the most benefit from this study guide, consider the following:

First, watch or listen to the program prior to working through the corresponding lesson in this guide. (Programs can also be viewed at **renner.org** by clicking on the Media/Archives links or on our Renner Ministries YouTube channel.)

Second, take the time to look up the scriptures included in each lesson. Prayerfully consider their application to your own life.

Third, use a journal or notebook to make note of your answers to each lesson's Study Questions and Practical Application challenges.

Fourth, invest specific time in prayer and in the Word of God to consult with the Holy Spirit. Write down the scriptures or insights He reveals to you.

Finally, take action! Whatever the Lord tells you to do according to His Word, do it.

For added insights on this subject, it is recommended that you obtain Rick Renner's books *The Holy Spirit and You: Working Together As Heaven's Dynamic Duo* and *Why We Need the Gifts of the Holy Spirit.* You may also select from Rick's other available resources, such as his book *Fallen Angels, Giants, Monsters, and the World Before the Flood,* by placing your order at **renner.org** or by calling 1-800-742-5593.

TOPIC

What Jesus Said About the Holy Spirit

SCRIPTURES

1. **John 14:16,17** — And I will pray the Father, and he shall give you another Comforter, that he may abide with you for ever; even the Spirit of truth; whom the world cannot receive, because it seeth him not, neither knoweth him: but ye know him; for he dwelleth with you, and shall be in you.

2. **John 14:26** — But the Comforter, which is the Holy Ghost, whom the Father will send in my name, he shall teach you all things, and bring all things to your remembrance, whatsoever I have said unto you.

3. **John 15:26** — But when the Comforter is come, whom I will send unto you from the Father, even the Spirit of truth, which proceedeth from the Father, he shall testify of me.

4. **John 16:7,8** — Nevertheless I tell you the truth; it is expedient for you that I go away: for if I go not away, the Comforter will not come unto you; but if I depart, I will send him unto you. And when he is come, he will reprove the world of sin, and of righteousness, and of judgment.

5. **John 16:13-15** — Howbeit when he, the Spirit of truth, is come, he will guide you into all truth: for he shall not speak of himself; but whatsoever he shall hear, that shall he speak: and he will shew you things to come. He shall glorify me: for he shall receive of mine, and shall shew it unto you. All things that the Father hath are mine: therefore said I, that he shall take of mine, and shall shew it unto you.

GREEK WORDS

1. "another" — ἄλλος (*allos*): another of the very same type; identical

2. "comforter" — παράκλητος (*parakletos*): a compound of παρά (*para*) and καλέω (*kaleo*); the word παρά (*para*) means alongside, and the

A Note From Rick Renner

I am on a personal quest to see a "revival of the Bible" so people can establish their lives on a firm foundation that will stand strong and endure the test as end-time storm winds begin to intensify.

In order to experience a revival of the Bible in your personal life, it is important to take time each day to read, receive, and apply its truths to your life. James tells us that if we will continue in the perfect law of liberty — refusing to be forgetful hearers, but determined to be doers — we will be blessed in our ways. As you watch or listen to the programs in this series and work through this corresponding study guide, I trust you will search the Scriptures and allow the Holy Spirit to help you hear something new from God's Word that applies specifically to your life. I encourage you to be a doer of the Word He reveals to you. Whatever the cost, I assure you — it will be worth it.

> Thy words were found, and I did eat them;
> and thy word was unto me the joy and rejoicing of mine heart:
> for I am called by thy name, O Lord God of hosts.
> — Jeremiah 15:16

Your brother and friend in Jesus Christ,

Rick Renner

The Ministry of the Holy Spirit for the New and Mature Believer

Copyright © 2024 by Rick Renner
1814 W. Tacoma St.
Broken Arrow, OK 74012-1406

Published by Rick Renner Ministries
www.renner.org

ISBN 13: 978-1-6675-0740-8

eBook ISBN 13: 978-1-6675-0741-5

word καλέω (*kaleo*) means to beckon or to call; as a compound, one who is called alongside; an advisor, advocate, or coach

SYNOPSIS

The five lessons in this study titled *The Ministry of the Holy Spirit for the New and Mature Believer* will focus on the following topics:

- What Jesus Said About the Holy Spirit
- 8 Things the Holy Spirit Does for Us
- The Holy Spirit — Our Supernatural Helper
- The Holy Spirit — Our Supernatural Indweller
- The Holy Spirit — Our Much-Needed Partner

What better person to explain who the Holy Spirit is and what He does in our lives than Jesus Himself? Before going to the Cross, He spent a great deal of time describing the Spirit's ministry in the life of all believers. As members of the Church who are living in these very last days, it is imperative that we learn who the Holy Spirit is and make room for His operation in and through our lives.

The emphasis of this lesson:

The Holy Spirit is not an "it" or an existential force hovering in the atmosphere. He is the Third Person of the Trinity who is fully God and identical in all ways to Jesus. He is our Comforter and the Spirit of Truth who leads and guides us into truth.

Jesus and the Holy Spirit Are One

On the very night Jesus shared the Last Supper and took communion with His disciples, He began to talk extensively about the ministry of the Holy Spirit. The apostle John records what Jesus said in chapters 14, 15, and 16. For three and a half years the disciples had connected in relationship with Him, but now He was going away, and the Holy Spirit was coming in His place. Therefore, it was vital that the disciples know and connect in relationship with the Holy Spirit.

When we look at the life of Jesus, we can clearly see that His life was entwined with the Holy Spirit from beginning to end. Consider these facts outlined in Scripture:

- Jesus was *conceived* by the Holy Spirit (*see* Luke 1:35).
- Jesus was *empowered* by the Holy Spirit (*see* Matthew 3:16).
- Jesus was *led* by the Holy Spirit (*see* Matthew 4:1).
- Jesus was *anointed* by the Holy Spirit to preach the Gospel and deliver captives (*see* Luke 4:18).
- Jesus *healed* people by the power of the Holy Spirit (*see* Acts 10:38).
- Jesus *cast out demons* by the power of the Holy Spirit (*see* Matthew 12:28).
- Jesus was *crucified* in the power of the Holy Spirit (*see* Hebrews 9:14).
- Jesus was *raised from the dead* by the Holy Spirit (*see* Romans 8:11).
- Jesus was *exalted to the Father's right hand* through the power of the Holy Spirit (*see* Ephesians 1:19,20).

Indeed, no one knew the Holy Spirit better than Jesus. His life was intimately intertwined with the Spirit, and at no time did Jesus rely on His own understanding. Instead, He remained totally dependent upon the Holy Spirit, cooperating and working together with Him in partnership. Whatever the Spirit said to do, Jesus did, and as a result, He was 100 percent successful.

Knowing that His disciples would accomplish nothing meaningful in their own natural abilities and strength, Jesus commanded them to remain in Jerusalem until they received the same empowerment from the Holy Spirit that He had received (*see* Luke 24:49; Acts 1:4,5).

The Holy Spirit Is a Person

It is interesting to note that throughout Jesus' teaching on the Holy Spirit in John's gospel, He never once calls the Spirit an "it," a "force," or a "feeling." Rather, Jesus refers to the Spirit 20 times using personal pronouns to describe Him. Consider what He said in John 14:16,17:

> **And I will pray the Father, and he shall give you another Comforter, that *he* may abide with you for ever; even the Spirit of truth; whom the world cannot receive, because it seeth *him* not, neither knoweth *him*: but ye know *him*; for *he* dwelleth with you, and shall be in you.**

In these two verses, Jesus uses five personal pronouns to describe the Holy Spirit. We see this again in John 14:26, where Jesus said:

> **But the Comforter, which is the Holy Ghost, whom the Father will send in my name, *he* shall teach you all things, and bring all things to your remembrance, whatsoever I have said unto you.**

Here, Jesus refers to the Holy Spirit as *He*, which is also how He refers to the Spirit in John 15:26:

> **But when the Comforter is come, whom I will send unto you from the Father, even the Spirit of truth, which proceedeth from the Father, *he* shall testify of me.**

Then when we come to John 16:7 and 8, we find that Jesus uses personal pronouns three more times in His description of the Holy Spirit. He said:

> **Nevertheless I tell you the truth; it is expedient for you that I go away: for if I go not away, the Comforter will not come unto you; but if I depart, I will send *him* unto you. And when *he* is come, *he* will reprove the world of sin, and of righteousness, and of judgment.**

Again, notice that Jesus didn't say, "I will send *it*," nor did He say, "I will send *a feeling* of spiritual goosebumps." He said, "I will send *Him* unto you," signifying that the Holy Spirit is a person.

The next mention of the Spirit is five verses later in John 16:13-15, where Jesus declared:

> **Howbeit when *he*, the Spirit of truth, is come, *he* will guide you into all truth: for *he* shall not speak of *himself*; but whatsoever *he* shall hear, that shall *he* speak: and *he* will shew you things to come. *He* shall glorify me: for *he* shall receive of mine, and shall shew it unto you. All things that the Father hath are mine: therefore said I, that *he* shall take of mine, and shall shew it unto you.**

If you go back and circle all the italicized words in these 3 verses, you will discover that there are 10 personal pronouns used to describe the Holy Spirit. If you add up the pronouns used in the 9 verses of all three chapters, you'll see there are 20 in all. The fact that Jesus used personal pronouns 20 times to describe the Holy Spirit means He is a *person*, and you can relate to Him just as you relate to the Father and to Jesus, the Son.

Remember, the Father is in Heaven, and Jesus is seated at His right hand on the throne (*see* Romans 8:34; Colossians 3:1). The Holy Spirit is the Third Person of the Trinity, and just as you talk to God and Jesus, you can speak to the Holy Spirit and pour your heart out to Him whenever and wherever you want (*see* Psalm 62:8).

The Holy Spirit Is Our 'Comforter'

Returning to Jesus' words in John 14:16 and 17, He said, "And I will pray the Father, and he shall give you another Comforter, that he may abide with you for ever; even the Spirit of truth...." There are two important words in this verse we really need to understand. The first is the word "another," which is the Greek word *allos*, and it means *another of the very same type* or one who is *identical*.

Up until that point, Jesus had been walking and working side-by-side with His disciples for three and a half years, and He had taught them how to teach and preach as well as how to heal the sick and cast out demons. By telling them the Father was going to give them "another" Comforter, Jesus was saying, "The Father is going to send you another (*allos*) Person who is identical to Me in every way."

Also notice the word "Comforter" — the marvelous Greek word *parakletos*. It is a compound of the word *para*, meaning *alongside*, and the word *kaleo*, which means *to beckon* or *to call*. When compounded to form *parakletos*, it describes *one who is called alongside*; one who serves as *an advisor, advocate*, or *coach*. That is the role Jesus played in the lives of His closest followers during His earthly ministry. He walked alongside them — counseling them, encouraging them, teaching them, and coaching them.

If you stop and think about it, Jesus advised and coached His disciples with everything pertaining to ministry. He told them what to take and how to pack their bags for traveling (*see* Mark 6:8,9). He also coached them on what to say when entering and exiting people's homes and what to do if a city didn't receive them (*see* Luke 10:5-11). Moreover, Jesus coached them on how to cast out demons and heal the sick (*see* Matthew 17:14-21).

Clearly, the disciples relied on Jesus for His coaching because He was alongside them all the time. But knowing He was about to leave earth, He reassured them that He would not leave them as orphans (*see* John 14:18 *NIV*). The Holy Spirit would be coming to take His place, and He would be *allos* — "another" identical to Jesus in every way.

Essentially, Jesus was telling them, "Everything I did for you when I was physically with you, the Holy Spirit will now do for you. He will coach you, advise you, teach you, and guide you in all things. Just as I taught you how to heal, cast out demons, and interact with people, the Holy Spirit will continue doing the very same things."

It is interesting to note that Jesus refers to the Holy Spirit as our "Comforter" four times in John's gospel: John 14:16, 26; 15:26; and 16:7. He repeatedly used this title to drive home this concept in His disciples' heart. They had physically related to Jesus for three and a half years, being able to see Him, touch Him, walk with Him, and talk with Him. Although they would not be able to physically interact with the Holy Spirit in these ways, the Spirit would come and continue to do everything that Jesus did for them.

The Holy Spirit Is the 'Spirit of Truth'

It is very likely that the disciples said, "But Jesus, how can we rely on and trust someone we cannot see?" In answer to their concerns, Jesus informed them that the Holy Spirit was not only their Comforter, but also the *Spirit of Truth*. He refers to the Spirit this way three times in John's gospel: John 14:17; 15:26; and 16:13.

This repeated emphasis was Jesus' way of saying, "Hey guys, the One who is coming after Me who is identical to Me can be fully trusted because He is the Spirit of Truth. He will never mislead you or misguide you. Anything He says to you, you can bank on it as being the truth, because He is the Spirit of Truth." Again, Jesus was trying to drive this perspective into the hearts of His followers.

He wants you to have the same understanding. The Holy Spirit is the Spirit of Truth in *your* life as well. Likewise, He is your Comforter who walks alongside you 24/7 — encouraging you, advising you, teaching you, and coaching you. He is a person, which is why Jesus used personal pronouns 20 times to paint a picture of who the Holy Spirit really is. He is not just a feeling of goosebumps or a force that surrounds and influences the world. He is the third Person of the Trinity who is fully God and lives inside all believers.

We can't develop a relationship with a "feeling" or a "force." But we can develop a relationship with a person! We can walk and talk with the Holy Spirit just like we do with God the Father and Jesus His Son. When the

Spirit talks to us and prompts us to do something, we should respond in obedience. He knows all things and will never lead us astray. Having this understanding is vital for new believers and mature believers alike.

QUESTIONS AND ANSWERS WITH RICK RENNER

In the program, Rick answered the following question from one of our viewers.

Q. What resort do you and Denise enjoy most in the world?"

A. "To be honest," Rick said, "My wife Denise and I don't do many vacations. If we go somewhere, we're going there to work or write a book. The resort we go to every day is described in Psalm 71:3 which says:

> **Be thou my strong habitation, whereunto I may continually resort....**

"My time with the Lord every morning is the greatest resort in the world! It is a getaway that you and I can go to every day — multiple times a day. It's a place where you'll be strengthened and refreshed, healed, and restored. In God's presence — the resort of all resorts — there is fullness of joy! (*See* Psalm 16:11.)

"Friend, I pray you discover the greatest resort on the planet — spending time in the Lord's presence. He is our strong habitation!"

STUDY QUESTIONS

> Study to shew thyself approved unto God, a workman that needeth not to be ashamed, rightly dividing the word of truth.
> — 2 Timothy 2:15

1. Jesus' life was intimately intertwined with the Holy Spirit, and at no time did He rely on His own understanding, which is what the Bible talks about in Proverbs 3:5-8. Take time to write out and commit to memory the powerful life-principle, and personalize it into a declaration you can speak over your life.

2. Knowing that His disciples would need the supernatural strength and power of the Holy Spirit, what did Jesus command them to do in Luke 24:49 and Acts 1:4 and 5. How did the Spirit manifest on the

Day of Pentecost (*see* Acts 2:1-12)? What effect did the infilling of the Holy Spirit have on Jesus' disciples? (Consider Acts 4:8-13, 31-33.)

3. What effects will the infilling of the Holy Spirit have in *your* life?

PRACTICAL APPLICATION

**But be ye doers of the word, and not hearers only,
deceiving your own selves.
— James 1:22**

1. Before going to the Cross, Jesus said, "And I will pray the Father, and he shall give you another Comforter..." (John 14:16). The word "another" means that the Holy Spirit is *another of the very same type* or One who is *identical* to Jesus. How does this truth expand your understanding of the person of the Holy Spirit? Does it create a greater desire for Him in your life?

2. According to Jesus, the Holy Spirit is your *Comforter* — your *Advisor, Counselor,* and *Coach* who walks alongside you. And He is also the *Spirit of Truth,* who leads you and guides you into all truth (*see* John 16:13). What do these two titles tell you personally about the Holy Spirit's work in *your* life? What might you do differently to benefit more from these roles He is called to fulfill?

3. Jesus remained totally dependent upon the Holy Spirit, cooperating and working with Him in partnership. Are *you* totally relying on the Holy Spirit for everything you need? If not, what areas in your life do you find yourself leaning on your own understanding and abilities? Take a few moments to acknowledge these things and commit them into the hands of the Holy Spirit, asking Him for the grace to trust Him more.

TOPIC
8 Things the Holy Spirit Does for Us

SCRIPTURES

1. **John 14:26** — But the Comforter, which is the Holy Ghost, whom the Father will send in my name, he shall teach you all things, and bring all things to your remembrance, whatsoever I have said unto you.

2. **John 15:26** — But when the Comforter is come, whom I will send unto you from the Father, even the Spirit of truth, which proceedeth from the Father, he shall testify of me.

3. **John 16:8** — And when he is come, he will reprove the world of sin, and of righteousness, and of judgment.

4. **John 6:44** — No man can come to me, except the Father which hath sent me draw him: and I will raise him up at the last day.

5. **2 Corinthians 5:21** — For he hath made him to be sin for us, who knew no sin; that we might be made the righteousness of God in him.

6. **John 16:13,14** — Howbeit when he, the Spirit of truth, is come, he will guide you into all truth: for he shall not speak of himself; but whatsoever he shall hear, that shall he speak: and he will shew you things to come. He shall glorify me....

GREEK WORDS

1. "teach"— **διδάσκω** (*didasko*): I teach; for one to be taught, he must be submitted to the teacher and see himself as an apprentice or a submitted learner who is willing to hear and obey whatever his master tells him to do

2. "all things"— **πάντα** (*panta*): all things; every little detail

3. "remembrance"— **ὑπομιμνῄσκω** (*hupomimnesko*): to put alongside one in order to remind him; to prompt one to remember

4. "reprove"— **ἐλέγχω** (*elegcho*): to expose, convict, or cross-examine for the purpose of conviction, as in convicting a lawbreaker in a court of law

5. "things to come"— **ἔρχομαι** (*erchomai*): whatever is to come

SYNOPSIS

In our first lesson, we learned an overview of what Jesus said about the Holy Spirit in chapters 14, 15, and 16 of John's gospel. Four times, He referred to the Spirit as our Comforter, which means He is *called alongside us* to serve as *an advisor, advocate*, and *coach*. Jesus also told us three times that the Holy Spirit is the *Spirit of Truth*, which means we can trust everything the Holy Spirit tells us.

Equally important is the fact that Jesus used personal pronouns 20 times in John 14, 15, and 16 to describe the Holy Spirit. This tells us that the Spirit of God is not a feeling or a force. Rather, He is a person with whom we can build a relationship. Specifically, He is the Third Person of the Godhead, and just as you can talk to the Father and Jesus, the Son, you can also talk to the Holy Spirit.

The Father is in Heaven, and Jesus is at His right hand praying for us (*see* Romans 8:34). It is the Holy Spirit who is present and active on the earth in this season of history. God poured out the gift of His Spirit upon His people — the Church — on the day of Pentecost (*see* Acts 2:1-4). And the same amazing Holy Spirit who filled believers in Jesus' day is still filling believers today!

The emphasis of this lesson:

Eight things the Holy Spirit will do for you as you partner with Him and receive His help include: (1) He teaches you; (2) He reminds you of things; (3) He testifies to you and through you; (4) He convicts you; (5) He convinces you of righteousness; (6) He guides you; (7) He reveals things to come; and (8) He worships Jesus with you.

As Our Comforter, the Holy Spirit *Coaches* Us

Looking once more at John 14:26, Jesus said, "But the Comforter, which is the Holy Ghost, whom the Father will send in my name, he shall teach you all things, and bring all things to your remembrance, whatsoever I have said unto you."

We saw that the word "Comforter" is the Greek word *paraklētos*, a compound of the words *para* and *klētos*. The word *para* means *alongside*, and the word *klētos*, which is from the word *kaléō*, means *to call* or *to beckon*.

When these words are compounded to form *paraklétos*, it means the Holy Spirit has been *called alongside us to regularly speak into our lives*. This word can also be translated as *helper, advocate, advisor, counselor*, or *coach*.

There are all sorts of coaches in our lives. Baseball players have baseball coaches who show each player things like how to throw the ball, catch the ball, and hit the ball. Those who sing have voice coaches, which is what Denise Renner had while she was in college. In any case, regardless of the kind of coach a person has, in order for that coach to be of help, the person must listen and then do what the coach says to do.

If your coach gives you instruction, and you refuse to listen — or you listen but choose not to do what he or she is telling you — even though the coach is right alongside you, their expertise is of no benefit because of your lack of cooperation.

Likewise, the Holy Spirit has been sent to us to be our Comforter. God the Father has called Him to walk alongside us and serve as our coach, instructing us in all things, including how to pray, how to witness and share the Good News, as well as what to say and what not to say in any conversation in which we find ourselves. But in order for the Holy Spirit's superior wisdom to benefit us, we have to listen to Him and willingly follow His directives.

#1: The Holy Spirit 'Teaches' Us

In addition to being our Comforter who coaches and advises us, John 14:26 identifies the Holy Spirit as our *Teacher*. The word "teach" in this verse is the Greek word *didasko*, which means *to teach*. Again, for a person to be taught, he must be submitted to the teacher and see himself as an apprentice or a submitted learner who is willing to hear and obey whatever his master tells him to do.

Friend, the Holy Spirit will teach you everything you need to know, when you need to know it. But in order for His teaching to be beneficial to you, you must have a submitted heart that is willing to do what He tells you.

#2: The Holy Spirit 'Reminds' Us

Jesus also said that the Holy Spirit will "bring all things to your remembrance" (John 14:26). The phrase "all things" is a translation of the Greek word *panta*, which means *all things; every little detail*. One of the jobs of the Holy Spirit as He walks alongside you is to bring every little detail you need to be aware of back to your *remembrance*.

In Greek, this word "remembrance" is *hupomimnesko*, and it means *to put alongside one in order to remind him* or *to prompt one to remember*. Whatever Jesus speaks to our spirit personally or reveals to us in His Word, the Holy Spirit will bring back to our remembrance.

A great example of the supernatural recall of the Holy Spirit is seen in the development of the four gospels. None of Jesus' disciples kept a diary of their daily activities with the Lord. So how did they remember everything that was said and done when the gospels were later penned? It was through the inspiration of the Holy Spirit. *He came alongside them and reminded them of Jesus' words and deeds.* He prompted them to remember every one of those events.

The same is true for you. If you trust the Holy Spirit, He will remind you of scriptures, prophetic words, and words of encouragement that were spoken to you. You can eliminate from your vocabulary the excuse, "I just can't remember" because the Holy Spirit will supernaturally remind you of scriptures, past events, people, and even errands you need to run. All you need to do is ask Him and trust Him to bring these things to your remembrance, and He will.

#3: The Holy Spirit 'Testifies' to Us and Through Us

The Holy Spirit has also been sent to testify to us and through us. In John 15:26, Jesus said, "But when the Comforter is come, whom I will send unto you from the Father, even the Spirit of truth, which proceedeth from the Father, he shall *testify* of me."

When the Holy Spirit comes powerfully into your life, He immediately begins to talk about Jesus! This becomes most evident when you sit to read and study the Scriptures. Since the Holy Spirit is the Author (*see* 2 Peter 1:20,21), He knows absolutely everything there is to know about every verse and how they point to Jesus. If you simply invite Him to reveal the Scriptures' meaning every time you open the Bible, He will testify of who Jesus is.

The more you know Jesus and are filled with His Spirit, the more you will want to testify to others about Him. In Acts 2, the 120 people in the Upper Room were filled with the Holy Spirit, and they boldly proclaimed the Gospel. As a result, 3,000 people were added to their number that day (*see* v. 41).

In Acts 4:13, Peter and John were brought before the Sanhedrin because of their bold proclamation of Jesus, and the elders and teachers of the Law were astonished at their boldness and took note that these two unlearned, ordinary men had been with Jesus. When the Holy Spirit is working in you, He will testify *to* you about Jesus and He will work *through* you to testify to others about Him.

#4: The Holy Spirit 'Convicts' Us

When we come to John 16:8, we discover more works of the Holy Spirit in our lives. Jesus said, "And when he is come, he will reprove the world of sin, and of righteousness, and of judgment." Notice the word "reprove." It is the Greek word *elegcho*, which means *to expose, convict, or cross-examine for the purpose of conviction, as in convicting a lawbreaker in a court of law.*

When a sinner hears the Word of God, the Word is so razor-sharp that it penetrates his soul as if he has been cross-examined on a witness stand. He is confronted with the reality of his sin until there is no denying it. This demonstrates the vital importance of partnering with the Holy Spirit when you share the message of Christ.

Without the work of the Holy Spirit testifying through us, we can speak to a sinner about their sin, and they will not be convicted. It is the convicting power of the Holy Spirit that illuminates truth and reveals one's sin. This is why Jesus said in John 6:44, "No man can come to me, except the Father which hath sent me draw him...." It is the Holy Spirit's job to convict sinners of their lost condition and show them their need for a savior.

#5: The Holy Spirit 'Convinces' Us of Righteousness

There is another work of the Spirit found in John 16:8, and it is to "reprove [believers] of righteousness." Again, the word "reprove" is the Greek word *elegcho*, which means *to expose, to convict,* or *to cross-examine for the purpose of conviction, as in convicting a lawbreaker in a court of law.*

Here we see that just as the power of the Holy Spirit is needed to wake up a sinner to his or her sin, the same supernatural power of the Spirit is also needed to convince a believer that he or she is righteous because of Jesus' finished work on the Cross.

> **For he hath made him to be sin for us, who knew no sin; that we might be made the righteousness of God in him.**
> **— 2 Corinthians 5:21**

The blood Jesus shed on the Cross as He took our sins upon Himself is what makes us righteous before God. May He be praised forever for His kindness!

For some believers, when they first hear this truth that God has made us righteous, it is very difficult to embrace because they are so conscious of their sinful nature that they struggle to grab hold of the truth that they have been declared righteous. Some struggle to even believe they are saved.

If you don't understand that you are righteous in Christ, ask the Holy Spirit to activate His convincing work in your life, helping you see beyond the shadow of any doubt that due to the blood of Jesus and His regenerative work, you have become the righteousness of God in Christ. Again, this is a supernatural work of the Holy Spirit.

#6: The Holy Spirit 'Guides' Us

Jesus went on to say, "Howbeit when he, the Spirit of truth, is come, he will guide you into all truth…" (John 16:13). Here we learn from Jesus that another role the Holy Spirit plays in our lives is to be our *guide*.

The word "guide" is the Greek word *hodegos*, which is a derivative of the word *hodos*, the Greek word for *a road*. When it becomes *hodegos*, like we find in this verse, it describes the Holy Spirit as *a tour guide*. And as our tour guide, the Holy Spirit knows all the right roads. He knows the ones we need to avoid and the ones that will be the most pleasurable to travel. Not only does He know the fastest route to our destination, but also the *safest* route.

The fact that Jesus likens the Holy Spirit to *a tour guide* means your Christian life is not supposed to be boring or monotonous. Instead, the Holy Spirit wants to take you on an adventure. He wants to lead you, guide you, and cause your Christian life to be adventuresome. Indeed, for the true believer who is actively pursuing the call of God on his or her life, there is never a dull moment!

#7: The Holy Spirit 'Reveals' Things to Come

What else did Jesus say the Holy Spirit would do in our lives? Again, we turn to His words in John 16:13, where He concludes by saying, "…He (the Holy Spirit) will shew you things to come." The phrase "things to come" is a translation of the word *erchomai*, and it means *whatever is to come.*

Although some people say this just refers to end-time biblical events (eschatology), that is not what Jesus is saying here. "Things to come" denotes *whatever is coming.* Remember, the Holy Spirit is your Coach, and your Coach doesn't just talk to you about theology. He will talk to you about practical matters such as where to live, what job to take, how to fix something that's broken, where to find something that's lost, and the best investments to make financially. Your Coach — the Holy Spirit — has the mind of God and knows everything about everything.

That said, "things to come" does include future events. If we are listening, the Holy Spirit will reveal to us difficult circumstances that are coming. We find an example of this in Acts 11:28 where a man named Agabus received a revelation from the Holy Spirit that an intense famine was coming that would affect the world, and it came to pass in the days of Claudius Caesar.

Later, when Paul was staying in the house of Philip the evangelist, Agabus came to him and told him of the future peril that awaited him in the city of Jerusalem (*see* Acts 21:8-11). Note that both examples deal with *personal* events, not theological doctrine. If we will ask and listen, the Holy Spirit will give us advance warning and reveal the attacks of the enemy, so we can cut him off and be victorious in all areas of our lives.

#8: The Holy Spirit 'Worships' Jesus With Us

The eighth activity we want to note in this lesson is that the Holy Spirit brings Jesus glory. Speaking of the Spirit, Jesus Himself said, "He shall glorify me…" (John 16:14). The Holy Spirit is a worshipper, and He loves to bring Jesus glory. As you develop a deeper relationship with the Spirit, He will help you to become freer in worship and praise. The more you yield to Him, the easier it is to lift your hands high, sing spiritual melodies, and even dance before the Lord in His presence.

As we wrap up this lesson, let's review the eight things the Holy Spirit will do for any Christian who partners with Him and receives His help:

(1) He teaches us; (2) He reminds us of things; (3) He testifies to us and through us; (4) He convicts us; (5) He convinces us of righteousness; (6) He guides us; (7) He reveals things to come; and (8) He worships Jesus with us.

In our next lesson, we will see how the Holy Spirit also functions as our Supernatural Helper.

QUESTIONS AND ANSWERS WITH RICK RENNER

In the program, Rick answered the following question from one of our viewers.

Q. What is the greatest thing you've ever done in ministry?

A. "God has done many amazing things in our ministry," Rick said. "If I were to compile a list of everything, it would be quite lengthy. I've actually documented a number of these things in my book *Unlikely*, which describes our unlikely journey of faith.

"That said, when I step back and look at everything we've done, there is one event that stands out among everything else, and that is the moment my wife, Denise, and I said *yes* to the will of God and moved our family to the Former Soviet Union. Everything else we have ever accomplished flowed out of that unified 'yes' to God's will.

"Friend, I want to encourage you to say *yes* to the Lord's will for your life today. That *yes* will change not only your life right now, but also everything in your future, and it will launch you into a journey and an adventure beyond your wildest imagination."

STUDY QUESTIONS

> Study to shew thyself approved unto God, a workman that
> needeth not to be ashamed, rightly dividing the word of truth.
> — 2 Timothy 2:15

1. One thing the Holy Spirit will do in our lives is teach us how to *testify* — that is, He will give us the right words to speak to anyone with whom we cross paths. Take some time to reflect on Matthew 10:19,20; Mark 13:11; and Luke 12:11,12. What promise does Jesus repeatedly make in these passages, and how do His words encourage you?

2. A major strategy of the enemy is to attack our mind with thoughts and feelings of *condemnation*. Jesus said the Holy Spirit counters this attack by convincing us that **we are righteous in Christ**. To fortify your mind in the fight against condemnation, take time to *regularly reflect* on these powerful promises, asking the Holy Spirit to bring them to your remembrance whenever needed.

   • John 3:17,18

   • Romans 8:1,2

   • Romans 8:33,34

   • 2 Corinthians 5:21

   • 1 John 3:19,20

PRACTICAL APPLICATION

**But be ye doers of the word, and not hearers only,
deceiving your own selves.
— James 1:22**

1. In order for the Holy Spirit's expert "coaching" to benefit you, you must *listen to Him* and choose to *do what He says*. Be honest — are you listening to the voice of the Holy Spirit? If you are, what has He been speaking to you lately? Are you doing what He tells you to do?

2. Jesus said the Holy Spirit will "bring all things to your remembrance" (John 14:26). This includes scriptures, past events, people, and tasks you need to do. The question is, are you asking the Holy Spirit to bring things to your remembrance? If not, begin to lean on Him for supernatural recall of whatever you need to remember.

3. Another thing Jesus said the Holy Spirit will do in your life is "…show you things to come" (*see* John 16:13), which means *whatever is coming*. Are you asking the Holy Spirit to reveal to you everything you need to know about what's coming — both the *spiritual* and the *practical* things? If you need direction on where to live, what job to take, how to fix something that's broken, where to find something that's lost, or what investments to make financially, ask the Holy Spirit for His wisdom on these things.

TOPIC

The Holy Spirit — Our Supernatural Helper

SCRIPTURES

1. **Romans 8:26** — Likewise the Spirit also helpeth our infirmities: for we know not what we should pray for as we ought: but the Spirit itself maketh intercession for us with groanings which cannot be uttered.

GREEK WORDS

1. "infirmities" — ἀσθένεια (*astheneia*): a generic word for all kinds of sicknesses and diseases

2. "disease" — νόσος (*nosos*): disease, but especially incurable or terminal disease

3. "disease or sickness" — μαλακίαν (*malakian*): crippling or debilitating disease

4. "grievously vexed" — κακῶς (*kakos*): bad or foul; used to depict those who are demonized and confused

5. "plague" — μαστιγός (*mastigos*): a scourge; a sickness that repeatedly strikes and strikes, again and again

6. "sick" — ἄρρωστος (*arroustos*): feeble, ill, or infirmed; comatose

7. "helpeth" — συναντιλαμβάνομαι (*sunantilambanomai*): σύν (*sun*), ἀντί (*anti*), and λαμβάνω (*lambano*); the word σύν (*sun*) means to do something in conjunction with another person; it connects you to someone else and paints the picture of two individuals working together; this is not one man trying to get the job done but two men working together to complete a task; thus, it pictures partnership and cooperation; the word ἀντί (*anti*) means against; the word λαμβάνω (*lambano*) means to take, to receive, or to take hold of something

8. "what" — τί (*ti*): pictures the most minute, minuscule detail; a very little thing

9. "as we ought" — δεῖ (*dei*): necessary or needful; refers to something that is obligatory

10. "intercession" — ὑπερεντυγχάνω (*huperentugchano*): to fall in with someone else; to meet in a circumstance or situation; to fall into with; to happen upon by accident; to meet with and to supplicate

11. "groanings" — στεναγμός (*stenagmos*): to aspirate; to vent; to release steam; to release great pressure

SYNOPSIS

As our "Comforter," the Holy Spirit has been called by God to indwell us and walk alongside us through every aspect of our life. When Jesus referred to the Holy Spirit as the Comforter, He was describing a practical relationship with the Holy Spirit that we can experience daily. We do not need to plead or beg for the Holy Spirit to come near because He is always *alongside* us.

The Spirit is with you throughout your entire day. He is with you when you pray, and He is with you when you don't pray. He is with you when you behave maturely, and He is with you through your moments of immaturity. He is with you when you go to work, to the movies, or to church. Everywhere you go, the Holy Spirit goes too, and in this lesson, we are going to learn how He functions as our *Supernatural Helper*.

The emphasis of this lesson:

When we face overwhelming circumstances and we don't know what to do, the Holy Spirit falls into the situation with us to tell us precisely what to pray. He is our Supernatural Helper who is right there with us, exerting His power and praying through us the exact, required prayer to bring about our rescue.

The Spirit Prays for Our 'Infirmities'

One of the most amazing passages of Scripture describing the partnership we have with the Holy Spirit is found in the eighth chapter of Romans. Under the inspiration of the Holy Spirit, the apostle Paul wrote:

> **Likewise the Spirit also helpeth our infirmities: for we know not what we should pray for as we ought: but the Spirit itself maketh intercession for us with groanings which cannot be uttered.**
>
> **— Romans 8:26**

Notice the latter part of the verse which says, "…The Spirit *itself* maketh intercession for us with groanings which cannot be uttered." The word "itself" is a poor translation. In Greek, it is the word *altos*, which would better be translated *himself.* The Holy Spirit is not an *it* or a thing; He is the Third Person of the Godhead who we can relate to personally.

Thus, "…The Spirit (*Himself*) maketh intercession for us with groanings which cannot be uttered" (Romans 8:26). The word "infirmities" here is the Greek word *astheneia*, which is a generic word for *all kinds of sicknesses and diseases.* In other words, "infirmities" (*astheneia*) encompasses a broad spectrum of ailments from the common cold to terminal cancer. Although you could say that individuals dealing with these ailments are both "sick," there's a big difference between a cold and cancer. Nevertheless, the Greek word *astheneia* can be used to describe both.

5 Primary Categories of Sicknesses in the New Testament

Now when you study the New Testament, you will discover that there are five primary categories of sicknesses that Jesus healed. All five of these fit inside the word *astheneia* — the all-inclusive word for "infirmities."

Category 1: *Nosos*

The first kind of sickness we find in the New Testament is indicated by the Greek word *nosos*. It is often translated as "disease," and it denotes *especially incurable or terminal disease.* An example of the use of this word is in Matthew 4:23 and 24. The word *nosos* would include AIDS as well as certain forms of cancer. Although these diseases were known to be incurable, Jesus healed people with them, and He is still healing people today.

Category 2: *Malakian*

The second category of sickness Jesus healed is denoted by the Greek word *malakian*, and it describes *a crippling or debilitating disease.* It is often translated as "disease" or "sickness" in the New Testament, and an example of this type is also found in Matthew 4:23 and 24. A person suffering with a *malakian* disease can live with it, but they can't function or get around very well because of its debilitating effects. Jesus healed those who were suffering from this kind of disease and is still healing people of this category of sickness today.

Category 3: *Kakos*

The third category of disease Jesus healed is denoted by the Greek word *kakos*. In the New Testament, this word is often translated as "grievously vexed" and was the result of demonic activity. The word *kakos* described a condition that was *bad* or *foul* and depicted *those who were demonized, confused*, and had mentally lost their way. Jesus healed those who suffered from this class of disease, and He is still healing people of it today.

Category 4: *Mastigos*

The fourth category of disease is one that may surprise you. It is often translated in the Scripture as "plague," and it is a translation of the Greek word *mastigos*. The most memorable example of this word *mastigos* is found in Mark 5 in the story of the woman who suffered with "an issue of blood" for 12 years. The word *mastigos* — translated as "plague" in Mark 5:29 — describes *a scourge* or *a sickness that repeatedly strikes and strikes, again and again.*

What is intriguing about the word *mastigos* is that it was used to describe a form of torture to which prisoners were subjected. A person who was incarcerated would be brought to the beating post, and they would strike him with a whip again and again and again. Once the prisoner's body was ripped open by the whip, he would be sent back to his cell.

Then just about the time that the man began to mend and feel better, they would bring him back to the beating post where they would pull out the whip and begin striking him again and again and again, reopening the wounds that were just beginning to heal. He was then sent back to his cell.

As time passed, his body began to heal, but just about that time, the torturers would return to repeat the beatings yet again — striking and striking and striking the prisoner. Although it was never severe enough to kill the man, the torture constantly kept him all torn up. That's what the word *mastigos* means and from where the word "plague" comes. Hence, a plague is any kind of sickness that repeatedly strikes and strikes and strikes you. Although it's not enough to kill you, it keeps you torn up all the time.

A more common example of this would include migraine headaches and arthritic joint pain. Just when you think you have gotten rid of it, *BAM!* It strikes you again with a vengeance, and while it doesn't kill you, the effects are so debilitating that you can often barely function. That's a plague — a *mastigos.*

Other examples include high blood pressure as well as chronic allergies. Just when you think you're over such a plague and you even give a praise report that you've been healed, it returns, striking and striking your physical body.

Athlete's feet or foot fungus is yet another example. After much prayer and the application of anti-fungal creams and oils, you think it's finally gone, but then it suddenly reappears and begins to strike you again and again. Regardless of what you do, you just can't seem to shake it. That's what a plague is — a *mastigos.*

This is what the woman with the issue of blood was dealing with for 12 years. Although she wasn't dead, she wasn't getting any better. The torturous sickness just kept lingering, draining her of her finances and her very life. Praise God that Jesus healed this category of sickness, and He's still healing it today!

Category 5: *Arroustos*

The fifth kind of disease in the New Testament is denoted by the word *arroustos*, and it is often translated as "sick." Individuals battling this form of sickness were *feeble, ill,* or *infirmed* to the extent that they had lost their strength and were homebound and bedfast. This word *arroustos* can even signify those who are *comatose.*

An example of this category of sickness is found in Mark 6 where it speaks of Jesus visiting His hometown of Nazareth. Because of their unbelief, "…he could there do no mighty work, save that he laid his hands upon a few sick folk, and healed them" (Mark 6:5). The word "sick" is the Greek word *arroustos*, and its use here indicates that when Jesus couldn't find conscious people who were willing to cooperate with Him, He searched for and found some comatose people He could heal. These individuals were so feeble and powerless that rather than resist Jesus, they willingly received His healing power.

The word *arroustos* is also used in Mark 16:18 where Jesus informs us that in His Name, "...(we) shall lay hands on the sick, and they shall recover." The word "sick" in this verse is the word *arroustos*, and its use here demonstrates how great our authority is in Jesus. Through faith in His Name, we can even lay our hands on those who are comatose, and they will recover!

In quick review, the five categories of sickness in the New Testament include (1) *nosos* — a terminal illness for which there's no natural cure; (2) *malakian* — a debilitating or crippling disease; (3) *kakos* — a demonized, mentally confused condition; (4) *mastigos* — a plague that repeatedly strikes again and again; and (5) *arroustos* — a feeble illness resulting in a weak, bedridden or comatose state. All these words fit inside the term *infirmities* in Romans 8:26.

What Do These Sicknesses Have To Do With You and the Holy Spirit?

It means that if you don't have the help of the Holy Spirit operating in your life, you are susceptible to each of these ailments.

Spiritually speaking, without the supernatural help of the Holy Spirit...

- You are *nosos* — your issues become terminal; you don't know how to help yourself nor does anyone else.

- You are *malakian* — you're spiritually debilitated and crippled.

- You are *kakos* — you're mentally and spiritually confused, oppressed by demonic influence.

- You are *mastigos* — your problems just keep beating and beating and beating you.

- You are *arroustos* — you become so spiritually feeble and weak you are homebound and comatose.

Without the supernatural help of the Holy Spirit, you don't know what to do or how to pray about the situation and circumstances you're facing. This applies to unbelievers as well as even Spirit-filled Christians. The fact is, even if you know the Bible and you know what it says about receiving healing and praying for others to be healed, that doesn't necessarily mean you know how to release healing to every single person who needs it.

It takes the unequaled wisdom and power of the Supernatural Helper — the Holy Spirit — working with you to effectively pray for yourself and every sick person with whom you come in contact. You need the Holy Spirit to coach you on how to pray, what to say, and what to do. When you ask Him, He will show you what to take authority over and what to cast out. The Holy Spirit sees what you do not see, and He knows what you do not know.

The Holy Spirit 'Helpeth' Our Infirmities

Looking once more at Romans 8:26, it says, "Likewise the Spirit also helpeth our infirmities: for we know not what we should pray for as we ought: but the Spirit itself maketh intercession for us with groanings which cannot be uttered."

The word "helpeth" in this verse is very important. It is the Greek word *sunantilambanomai*, which is a compound of three words: *sun*, *anti*, and *lambano*. The word *anti* means *against*, and the word *lambano* means *to take*, *to receive*, or *to take hold of something*. These words speak of how the Holy Spirit is against our infirmities and knows how to take hold of them.

This brings us to the word *sun*, which means *to do something in conjunction with another person*. It connects you to someone else and paints the picture of *two individuals working together*. Thus, it is not just you trying to get the job done alone. It is you AND the Holy Spirit working together to complete a task.

In this case, the Holy Spirit joins Himself to us, and we face every issue with him. He knows the root of every problem, and He knows exactly how to deal with them and pray about them to see them resolved. Hence, the word *sun* pictures *partnership* and *cooperation*.

We Don't Know 'What' To Pray

The biggest challenge we have is stated clearly in this verse: "…For we know not what we should pray…" (Romans 8:26). The words "we know not" mean we *lack the know-how*, and it underscores our ignorance and our need for help. This happens to everyone, even the most seasoned intercessors. There are times when we simply do not know how to pray.

All of us have probably been confronted with a crisis where we had to make a decision but didn't have any idea how to handle the situation. This is part of our weak, human condition — and one of the things that the

Holy Spirit comes to remove. He grabs that ignorance, removes it, and gives us the "know-how" when it comes to praying.

When the Bible says, "…For we know not *what* we should pray…" (Romans 8:26), the word "what" is the little Greek word *ti*, and it pictures *the most minute, minuscule detail* or *a very little thing*. The use of the word *ti* here tells us **we know not** the most minute, minuscule detail of what we are to pray.

Yes, we may know what the Word of God says about healing, but having a general knowledge of healing and understanding the *specific, minute details* of what we are to pray in a given situation are two very different things. We know it's God's will to heal everyone, but unless the Holy Spirit — the Supernatural Helper — joins together with us and removes the obstacles of ignorance, we won't know the specific details of what a person is dealing with nor how to pray specifically for them to be healed.

Only the Holy Spirit knows *why* a person is sick. Only He can see if the root cause is a lesion on the person's brain or if it is offense and unforgiveness in the person's heart. Only He knows if the disease they are facing is the result of a chemical imbalance, demonic influence, or a combination of both. On our own, we don't know any of these things.

So, while we can pray a general prayer based on general knowledge of God's Word, and it is good, it is merely a shot in the dark. It is the Holy Spirit who knows the root of our problem and has the ability to zoom in on it and fix it. He knows how to pray, what to bind, and what to rebuke. On our own, we lack the know-how.

The Holy Spirit 'Maketh Intercession' for Us

Again, Romans 8:26 says, "…For we know not what we should pray for as we ought…." The phrase "as we ought" is a translation of the Greek word *dei*, which means *as is necessary or needful* and refers to *something that is obligatory*. This tells us that there is a required, necessary way to pray for every situation. It is wrong to think that "one prayer fits all" situations and circumstances. We need to pray specifically if we want to see results.

The Holy Spirit is the only one who knows how to pray exactly what's required in each situation. That is why we need to unite with Him in partnership when we pray. He is our Supernatural Helper, which is what the remainder of Romans 8:26 reveals.

...But the Spirit itself maketh intercession for us with groanings which cannot be uttered.

The word "intercession" in this passage is the Greek word *huperentugchano*, which means *to fall in with someone else*. The use of this word here tells us that when you feel you're stuck in a difficult place where you don't know what to do or what to pray, that's the moment for you to say, "Holy Spirit, You're my Coach, and I need you to join me where I am. Fall in with me in this situation." And the Holy Spirit who is your Helper (*sun*), will connect Himself to you.

Additionally, the word *huperentugchano* — translated here as "intercession" — paints the picture of someone coming across a person who has fallen into a pit. Upon discovering the trapped person, he immediately goes into the pit with him to "supplicate" for him, which means to *rescue* him. To "supplicate" for someone means you're delivering him or her from imminent danger. You are snatching the person and pulling him out. That is exactly what Romans 8:26 says the Holy Spirit does for us.

Sadly, when many believers fall into a trap of the enemy, they become fretful, anxious, and they give up hope. They are depressed, disgusted, and confused, and they don't know how they are going to get out of the mess they are in. Because they are too busy worrying and fretting about what has happened to them, they become incapacitated by their situation.

What they don't realize is that the Holy Spirit fell into the ditch with them and that they do not have to deal with the challenge by themselves. He is by their side and has already begun supplicating for them. In fact, the moment they fell, He started putting together a rescue plan to get them out of the mess.

It's as if the Holy Spirit is saying, "Hey, I'm here. I'm going to wrap one arm around you and use My other arm to push against the obstacle. Together, we are going to press against it until it moves. I know you're worried about the money, about the conflict, about that sickness; but together, we are going to push against this obstacle until it is out of the way."

Through Your Prayers
the Holy Spirit Releases His Power

When you ask for help, the Holy Spirit goes to work! But the Spirit needs a vessel He can pray through. He needs *you* to give voice to the prayers.

Again, the Bible says, "...But the Spirit itself maketh intercession for us with groanings which cannot be uttered" (Romans 8:26). The word "groanings" is the Greek word *stenagmos*, which means *to aspirate*, *to vent*, *to release steam*, or *to release great pressure*.

An example of this word *stenagmos* would be how a teapot on the stove reacts when the flame has been turned up under it. Eventually, the heat of the fire causes the water inside to boil. The pressure builds, and soon steam shoots from the kettle, causing the teapot to whistle.

Steam is powerful. In fact, it is so strong it can move mighty trains down a track and move huge ships across the seas. Likewise, when the Holy Spirit begins to release His power in your life, He releases divine energy to move obstacles and the enemy out of the way. Whether it's sickness, divisiveness in relationships, financial lack, or another type of demonic attack, the Holy Spirit's power is greater than anything that comes against you.

When we have fallen into a pit, it often feels as though our world is falling apart. It may look as though we are about to fail, but when we cry out, **"HELP ME, HOLY SPIRIT!"** He falls into the situation with us and begins to go to work in us and on our behalf. Little by little, the spiritual pressure builds and builds and builds until, finally, it explodes. When it explodes, the Holy Spirit vents spiritual steam, and incredible prayers rise up from the inside of us. The Bible describes this as "groanings which cannot be uttered."

Friend, if you feel like you're trapped in a pit, cry out to the Holy Spirit for help! Ask Him to fall into the situation with you, eradicate your inability and ignorance, and show you what to pray and do in the situation.

QUESTIONS AND ANSWERS WITH RICK RENNER

In the program, Rick answered the following question from one of our viewers.

Q. Was the apostle Paul mentally ill before he came to Christ?

A. The Bible does not implicitly say that Paul was mentally ill, but there are clues that lead us to believe he had a mental issue and was also eaten up with hate.

The reason we believe this is because of his own words in First Timothy 1:13. He said that before he came to Christ, he was a *blasphemer*, a *persecutor*, and *injurious.* Essentially, that word "injurious" describes *one who derives pleasure from inflicting pain on others.*

Add to this the description in Acts 8:3 of what Paul (then called Saul) was doing before surrendering to Jesus. The Bible says he "…made havock of the church, entering into every house, and haling men and women committed them to prison." The word "havock" is the very word that was used to describe *diseased pigs that came into villages and mauled people.* This is the word the Holy Spirit prompted Luke to use to describe Paul before he came to Christ.

So when you consider the words *injurious* and *havoc* that are used to describe Paul, we can certainly determine that mentally, he was eaten up with hate before he came to Christ.

STUDY QUESTIONS

Study to shew thyself approved unto God, a workman that needeth not to be ashamed, rightly dividing the word of truth.
— 2 Timothy 2:15

1. Were you aware that there are five different categories of sickness in the New Testament? How does this knowledge change the way you view disease and Jesus' supernatural power to heal?
2. Have you or someone close to you experienced physical healing? What category of sickness were you (he or she) dealing with, and how did God bring about the healing?
3. One type of sickness Jesus healed is referred to as a "plague" — the Greek word *mastigos.* This is any kind of sickness that *repeatedly strikes you again and again,* and although it's not enough to kill you, it keeps you torn up all the time. Are you dealing with a disease of this nature? If so, what is it? To strengthen your faith and believe for your healing, read through the story of the woman "plagued" (*mastigos*) with the issue of blood (*see* Matthew 9:20-22; Mark 5:24-34; Luke 8:43-48).

PRACTICAL APPLICATION

But be ye doers of the word, and not hearers only, deceiving your own selves.
— James 1:22

1. As you come to the end of this lesson, what is your greatest takeaway?
2. Are you in a situation where you don't know how or what to pray? Take time to briefly describe what you're walking through. As you yield yourself to the Holy Spirit and seek Him for help, consider God's promises found in Psalm 25:9,12; 32:8; 73:24; Isaiah 30:21; James 1:5.
3. If you feel you're stuck and you need to know what to do and what to pray, say, "**Help me, Holy Spirit!** You're my Coach, and I need You to join me where I am. Fall into this situation with me. Use my mouth to vent 'spiritual steam' and release Your explosive power through my prayers. In Jesus' name!"

LESSON 4

TOPIC

The Holy Spirit — Our Supernatural Indweller

SCRIPTURES

1. **James 4:4,5** — Ye adulterers and adulteresses, know ye not that the friendship of the world is enmity with God? whosoever therefore will be a friend of the world is the enemy of God. Do ye think that the scripture saith in vain, The spirit that dwelleth in us lusteth to envy?

GREEK WORDS

1. "friendship" — φιλία (*philia*): friendship, affection, attraction, fondness, or love; an intense fondness that is developed between people who enjoy each other's company; two or more people who know one another, who are fond of one another, and who are growing more deeply involved in each other's lives; a reciprocal relationship
2. "world" — κόσμος (*kosmos*): the world; depicts anything fashioned or ordered; denotes systems and institutions in society, such as fashion, finances, education, and entertainment; world systems
3. "enmity" — ἐχθρός (*echthros*): hatred; hostility; an enemy or opponent; animosity, antagonism, or enmity; describes those who are irreconcilable;

depicts enemies in a military conflict or hostile enemies; used to describe the antagonistic relationship between Pontius Pilate and Herod Antipas

4. "will be" — βούλομαι (*boulomai*): to counsel or to resolve

5. "friend" — φίλος (*philos*): a beloved friend; dear; friendly; a companion; an associate; held dear in a close bond of affection; a reciprocal relationship

6. "is" — καθίστημι (*kathistemi*): to constitute, to make, or to render

7. "enemy" — ἐχθρός (*echthros*): hatred; hostility; an enemy or opponent; animosity, antagonism, or enmity; describes those who are irreconcilable; depicts enemies in a military conflict or hostile enemies; used to describe the antagonistic relationship between Pontius Pilate and Herod Antipas

8. "the spirit" — τὸ πνεῦμα (*to pneuma*): the definite article τό (*to*) with the word πνεῦμα (*pneuma*), which means spirit; this clearly means James was referring to the Holy Spirit; thus, James was describing the residency of the Holy Spirit in the life of a believer

9. "dwelleth" — κατοικέω (*katoikeo*): depicts settling down into a home; a permanent resident

10. "in" — ἐν (*en*): in or inside

11. "lusteth" — ἐπιποθέω (*epipotheo*): an intense desire; a craving, a hunger, an ache, a yearning, or a hankering for something; a longing or pining for something; to strain after; to greatly desire; to have strong affection; a fervent passion; an obsession

12. "envy" — φθόνος (*phthonos*): jealousy; a hostile feeling toward someone else because of an advantage, benefit, or position that another has; a deeply felt grudge due to someone possessing what one wishes was his own

SYNOPSIS

What happens the moment you repent of your sins and invite Jesus to be your Lord and Savior? His Spirit moves in and takes up residence in your life (*see* John 14:23). Paul says repeatedly that your body is the temple of the Holy Spirit, and you belong to Him (*see* 1 Corinthians 6:19). He loves you passionately and is jealous for your love and attention. The question is: Are you giving Him His place of preeminence, or are you giving your love and attention to the things of this world?

The emphasis of this lesson:

As our Supernatural Indweller, the Holy Spirit longs for and deeply craves our love and attention. We must guard our hearts from falling in love with the things of the world and making anything a higher priority than God. In His eyes, this is spiritual adultery and positions us as His hostile enemy.

Believers Can Commit Spiritual Adultery

The book of James was written by James, the half-brother of Jesus. He wrote to Jews who had converted to Christianity after hearing and receiving the Good News of Jesus, the long-awaited Messiah, and had been dispersed across the Roman Empire. For various reasons, these new believers were struggling in their relationship with the Lord. So much so, that James wrote to them and said:

> Ye adulterers and adulteresses, know ye not that the friendship of the world is enmity with God? whosoever therefore will be a friend of the world is the enemy of God.
>
> —James 4:4

Now, understand that Jewish believers did not commit adultery. In fact, before these individuals came to Christ, as Jews, if they had committed adultery, they could have been stoned to death for their actions. So, for James to call them *adulterers* and *adulteresses* was like a slap in the face. It was a highly degrading insult that certainly must have stunned them.

Apparently, they had crossed a line and were doing something so foul that James felt the need to correct them.

What is interesting is that when you dive into the Greek text, it just says *adulteresses*. The reason is because he was referring to the Bride of Christ. Spiritually speaking, Jesus is the Groom, and the Church collectively is called His Bride. At the time of James' writing, his readers were in some way committing spiritual adultery, which is why he called them adulteresses.

'Friendship With the World' Is Adultery in God's Eyes

James then asks, "…Know ye not that the friendship of the world is enmity with God?" (James 4:4) A better translation of this part of the verse in the Greek would be, "Don't you know? Have you not yet comprehended? Have you not yet grasped that the friendship of the world is enmity with God." It's as if James is reaching through the pages of his letter to shake his readers and say, "What in the world are you doing?"

The word "friendship" here is the Greek word *philia*, which describes *friendship, affection, attraction, fondness*, or *love*. It is *an intense fondness that is developed between people who enjoy each other's company*. This is two or more people who know one another, who are fond of one another, and who are growing more deeply involved in each other's lives. The word *philia* depicts *a reciprocal relationship*.

This brings us to the word "world," which is the Greek word *kosmos*, and it depicts *the world* or *anything fashioned or ordered*. Thus, it denotes systems and institutions in society, such as fashion, finances, education, entertainment, or any kind of world system. It seems the believers James was addressing had begun to fall in love with the things of the world. Their attention, affection, and attraction to entertainment, fashion, business, and other worldly affairs were becoming greater and competing with their love and devotion to God.

James said their misplaced affection for the world was "enmity with God" (James 4:4). In Greek, the word "enmity" is *echthros*, which describes *hatred* or *hostility* and can depict *an enemy* or *opponent*. It is the idea of *animosity, antagonism*, or *enmity*, and it describes *those who are irreconcilable*. This word *echthros* can also depict enemies in a military conflict or hostile enemies. It is the very word used in the gospels to describe the antagonistic relationship between Pontius Pilate and Herod Antipas.

The fact that James used this word *echthros* — translated "enmity" — tells us clearly that God and the unbelieving world are never going to be reconciled. He is at enmity with the lost world because it is hostile toward Him.

Apparently, the Christians James was addressing — who had the Spirit of God living inside them — had begun to enter a reciprocal relationship with the things of the world. In God's eyes, it was spiritual adultery, and James took them to task about it, telling them in no uncertain terms that it wasn't right.

Beware of Talking Yourself Into Loving the World and Falling Out of Love With God

James 4:4 wraps up by saying, "…Whosoever therefore will be a friend of the world is the enemy of God." Once more, we see the word "friend" — the Greek word *philos*. Here it describes *a beloved friend, a dear friend*, or *one that is friendly*. It can also denote *a companion, an associate*, or *one held dear in a close bond of affection*. Like the word "friendship" used earlier in the verse, the word "friend "(*philos*) also depicts *a reciprocal relationship*.

What James is telling us here is that when you enter a reciprocal relationship with the world and you're growing more and more deeply in love with the things of the world, it puts you in a bad place with God. In fact, it makes you God's *enemy*.

How does a follower of Christ transition into such a precarious place? Look again at James 4:4, which says, "…Whosoever therefore *will be* a friend of the world is the enemy of God." Notice the important words "will be" — they are a translation of the Greek word *boulomai*, which means *I counsel* or *I advise*. Normally, when people need direction, they seek out a counselor for advice. In this verse, the word *boulomai* carries the idea of a believer who is *counseling himself*, assuring himself that it is perfectly acceptable to be a friend of the world.

What we are seeing in this passage is a picture of how Christians backslide. It doesn't happen overnight — it is a process. Little by little, the allurements of this world along with the seductive voice of the enemy begin to capture the attention of a believer to such an extent that they start talking themselves into compromising their devotion to Jesus. One exception here leads to another exception there, and then to another and another and another. Slowly, almost imperceptibly, they counsel themselves out of the red-hot devotion to the Lord and into a relationship with the world. God calls people who do this His enemy.

Once you compromise one time and give in to the ways of the world, it is easier to do it again and again. With each additional wrong choice that embraces the world, the heart becomes more and more callous and less sensitive to the still small voice of the Holy Spirit and His conviction about the wrong things you are doing. Again, this is how believers backslide — little by little, choice by choice.

What Does It Mean To Be God's 'Enemy?'

So according to James 4:4, whoever is a friend of the world — whoever is *a companion, an associate,* or *holds a close bond of affection* with the world's systems — he or she "...*is* the enemy of God." Interestingly, even the word "is" has significance. It is the Greek word *kathistemi,* and it means *to constitute oneself, to make oneself,* or *to render oneself.* Hence, this movement from being a friend of God to being an enemy of God is *self-induced.*

The word "enemy" is again the Greek word *echthros,* which describes *hatred, hostility, an enemy,* or *an opponent.* It is the picture of *animosity, antagonism,* or *enmity,* and it describes *those who are irreconcilable.* This word *echthros* is used in the New Testament to depict the hostile, antagonistic relationship between Pontius Pilate and Herod Antipas.

It's use in this verse means that when a Christian enters a reciprocal relationship with the world — and the world becomes the object of his fondness and affection instead of the Lord who rightfully deserves it — his wrong choices render him to be in an antagonistic, hostile position with God.

When we insert the original Greek meaning of all these words, we have the *Renner Interpretive Version* (*RIV*) of James 4:4, which says:

> **You adulteresses! Don't you understand very clearly that a reciprocal relationship and friendship with the world — and being enmeshed in its affairs — puts you in an adversarial and hostile position with God? If then, anyone — and I really mean** *anyone* **— has talked himself into believing that it's all right to be a companion in a reciprocal relationship with the world, that person, by his wrong choices, has made himself to be an enemy of God. His choices and actions have put him into a position that is contrary to and hostile to God.**

The Holy Spirit Has Made You His Forever Home

Understanding the meaning of James 4:4 makes the meaning of James 4:5 much clearer and more meaningful. In this verse, James goes on to say:

> **Do ye think that the scripture saith in vain, The spirit that dwelleth in us lusteth to envy?**

Notice the words "the spirit." They are a translation of the Greek words *to pneuma*, which is the definite article *to* coupled with the word *pneuma*, the word for *spirit*. Because the definite article *to* appears, we know James was referring to THE Holy Spirit. Thus, he is describing the residency of the Holy Spirit in the life of a believer.

He says the Spirit "dwelleth in us," and the word "dwelleth" is the Greek word *katoikeo*, which is a compound of the word *kata*, meaning *down*, and the word *oikos*, the Greek term for a *house*. When these two words are compounded to form the word *katoikeo*, it depicts *settling down into a home* or becoming *a permanent resident*. The use of *katoikeo* here tells us that when the Holy Spirit comes into our life at the moment of our new birth in Christ, He doesn't come and go like a guest staying in a hotel. Instead, He takes up *permanent residency*.

Just imagine! When the Spirit of God came into your heart, it's as if He rolled out His own carpets, set up His own easy chair, hung His own pictures on the wall, and settled down inside you. He felt so good when He entered your life, He said, "I'm going to stay here forever! I have become a permanent indweller in this person's heart."

Friend, our heart is the Holy Spirit's home, and He has settled down inside us. He literally indwells us, and not only does He indwell us, but James also says He is *in* us. That word "in" in James 4:5 is the "in" of *inside*, which is where the Holy Spirit lives — right on the inside of us!

The Holy Spirit Wants You All to Himself

After informing us that the Holy Spirit has made Himself at home and is permanently living inside us, James then says that the Spirit "…lusteth to envy" (James 4:5). This strange word "lusteth" is the Greek word *epipotheo*, which is a compound of the words *epi* and *potheo*. The word *epi* is an intensifier, and the word *potheo* means *to yearn for* or *hanker for*. When these words come together to form *epipotheo*, it describes *an intense desire; a craving, a hunger, an ache, a yearning*, or *a hankering for something*.

What is the Holy Spirit craving and longing for? YOU! He is pining for, straining after, and greatly desiring your attention and total devotion. He yearns for Jesus to be your chief focus. The moment you surrender your life to God, His Spirit enters and takes up residence in you. As you yield to Him, He begins filling you with Himself and sanctifying your life. Regardless of what you yield to Him today, He will ask for more of you tomorrow and the next day and the day after that.

Make no mistake:

The Holy Spirit wants you and *all of you*!

Along with His strong affection, fervent passion, and obsession for you, the Bible says the Spirit of God has *envy*. In Greek, the word "envy" is *phthonos*, which describes *jealousy* or *a hostile feeling toward someone else because of an advantage, benefit, or position that another has*. Moreover, it is a deeply felt grudge due to someone possessing what one wishes was his own.

So James 4:4 and 5 is a picture of believers who were at one time madly in love with Jesus, but now they have talked themselves into walking backward into a relationship with the world. Consequently, their fondness and affection has moved from Jesus to the world.

Although the Holy Spirit has settled down inside us and become a permanent indweller, He does not demand or force us to give Him attention. Instead, He longs, yearns, and pines for us to pursue Him and give Him our affection. If we fail to do so and fall in love with the world instead, He considers it an act of spiritual adultery.

Taking into account the original Greek meaning, here is the *Renner Interpretive Version (RIV)* of James 4:5:

> **Do you suppose the scripture says to no purpose that the Spirit has settled down, taken up residency, and permanently dwells inside us and is filled with an intense jealously anytime we give our devotion to someone or something else. In fact, the Holy Spirit so passionately pines and yearns for us [that He is not willing to share us or for us to share our highest devotion with anyone or anything else more than Him].**

Of course, this doesn't mean you can't work hard at your job, have material possessions, or enjoy things in this life. It just means that the things of this life must take a back seat to our devotion to the Lord. Pursuing Him, loving Him, and giving Him our first and best is what the Holy Spirit longs for, and He is not willing for anything or anyone else to be a substitute for Him.

Friend, you can have nice things, but don't let those things have you. Your heart belongs to the Holy Spirit and Him alone. You are His home. He loves you passionately and has taken up permanent residency inside of you. He yearns for your time, your attention, and your loving devotion. As you open your life to His presence, He will completely possess you and sanctify every area of your life for His glory!

QUESTIONS AND ANSWERS WITH RICK RENNER

In the program, Rick answered the following question from one of our viewers.

Q. Who was the first prophet in the Old Testament?

A. According to Jewish rabbis, the first official prophet in the Old Testament was *Enoch*, the great-great-great-great grandson of Adam. We read about him in Genesis 5:21-24, which tells us that he walked with God so closely that one day the Lord just decided to take him directly to Heaven, without him experiencing death. This was the first official rapture recorded in Scripture.

Enoch was so admired by the Early Church that Jude, the half-brother of Jesus, quoted him in his writings. Citing Enoch's prophetic vision of the Second Coming of Christ, Jude wrote:

> **And Enoch also, the seventh from Adam, prophesied of these, saying, Behold, the Lord cometh with ten thousands of his saints, to execute judgment upon all, and to convince all that are ungodly among them of all their ungodly deeds which they have ungodly committed, and of all their hard speeches which ungodly sinners have spoken against him.**
>
> **— Jude 1:14,15**

This passage informs us that at the very outset of time, Enoch was so spiritually attuned that he saw the very end of all the ages and prophesied about the Second Coming of Jesus. The fact that God gave Enoch — who lived more than 5,000 years ago — the divine ability to see what was going to happen at the very end of the age helps us see why he was considered the first official prophet in the Old Testament.

STUDY QUESTIONS

> Study to shew thyself approved unto God, a workman that
> needeth not to be ashamed, rightly dividing the word of truth.
> — 2 Timothy 2:15

1. Anything in our life that we give *more* attention, admiration, or
    affection to than God, He considers an *idol*. What does God think
    of idols? Check out what He Himself says in Exodus 20:1-6; 34:14;
    Leviticus 26:1; Deuteronomy 5:7-10; and Isaiah 42:8. And to let us
    know His feelings haven't changed, He says in this New Testament
    passage:

    **Little children, keep yourselves from idols (false gods) — [from
    anything and everything that would occupy the place in your
    heart due to God, from any sort of substitute for Him that
    would take first place in your life]. Amen (so let it be).**
    — 1 John 5:21 *AMPC*

    What is the Holy Spirit speaking to you personally in these passages?
2. The greatest desire of God's heart is also the greatest commandment ever
    given. God spoke it through Moses in Deuteronomy 6:4,5, and Jesus
    declared it again in Matthew 22:36-38; Mark 12:28-30; Luke 10:27.
    What is this all-time, number one commandment?

PRACTICAL APPLICATION

> But be ye doers of the word, and not hearers only,
> deceiving your own selves.
> — James 1:22

1. Be honest with God and yourself: Are you giving Him His place of
    preeminence? Is He top priority and your driving passion? Ask the
    Holy Spirit (and yourself), "Where is most of my time and attention
    going? What fills my calendar? Do I really want to know God, be in
    His Word and presence, and accomplish His will? Or am I attracted
    more to entertainment, business, fashion, sports, and other affairs of
    life?" Be still and listen. What do you sense the Holy Spirit saying?
2. According to the original Greek meaning of James 4:4, the way a
    believer backslides and becomes an enemy of God is by *counseling
    himself* (*boulomai*) to be a friend of the world. Has that ever happened

to you? Is it happening to you right now? Are you talking to yourself, reassuring yourself that it's okay to participate in certain things that you know grieve God's heart? If you recognize this pattern in your life, repent and do what Jesus said to do in Revelation 2:4,5.

3. If you feel like your priorities are out of whack, your love for Christ has dwindled, and your affection for the things of this world has increased, pray: "Father, please forgive me for being more attracted and interested in the things of this world than with You (*name anything specific that the Holy Spirit reveals as an idol*). I don't want to continue going down that path, but I need Your help. Purify my heart and help me fall in love with You all over again. In Jesus' name."

LESSON 5

TOPIC

The Holy Spirit — Our Much-Needed Partner

SCRIPTURES

1. **2 Corinthians 13:14** — The grace of the Lord Jesus Christ, and the love of God, and the communion of the Holy [Spirit], be with you all. Amen.

2. **Galatians 2:9** — And when James, Cephas, and John, who seemed to be pillars, perceived the grace that was given unto me, they gave to me and Barnabas the right hands of fellowship....

3. **Matthew 6:6** — But thou, when thou prayest, enter into thy closet, and when thou hast shut thy door, pray to thy Father which is in secret; and thy Father which seeth in secret shall reward thee openly.

4. **Luke 5:7** — And they beckoned unto their partners, which were in the other ship, that they should come and help them....

5. **Philippians 4:14** — Notwithstanding ye have well done, that ye did communicate with my affliction.

GREEK WORDS

1. "communion" — κοινωνία (*koinonia*): fellowship; partnership; responsibility

2. "closet" — ταμεῖον (*tameion*): a secret place where one would hide his most valuable possessions; a secure place like a safety deposit box, where your priceless possessions were kept under lock and key; eventually came to describe a place like a bank where you could keep your money so it would be safe; by Early New Testament times, the word "closet" evolved again and came to describe a bedroom

SYNOPSIS

We began our series by establishing the fact that the Holy Spirit is not an "it," a "feeling," or a "force." He is a *person* — the Third Person of the Trinity who is fully God and who we are privileged to interact with on the earth today. He wants us to learn to relate to Him as a person and to enjoy fellowship with Him daily. He is our Comforter, our Supernatural Helper, and our Supernatural Indweller who does countless extraordinary things in our lives. In this lesson, we will see how the Holy Spirit is also our much-needed Partner who wants to commune with us daily and take full responsibility for our lives.

The emphasis of this lesson:

Communion with the Holy Spirit is the highest level of intimacy we can have with Him. This communion is an invitation into His inner circle to fellowship with Him, partner with Him, and entrust Him to take responsibility of our life.

'I Was Looking for More Than Just a Feeling'

Are you wanting to know God more? Are you seeking to better understand who the Person of the Holy Spirit is and how we are to interact with Him on a daily basis? That is what Rick Renner was searching for many years ago when he was a teenager. He shared this story of how his hunger led him to discover the Holy Spirit in ways he would have never imagined:

> When I was a teenager, I became really hungry for the things of God, and I ended up baptized in the Holy Spirit and began

speaking with other tongues. Suddenly, it was like a whole new spiritual world opened to me.

Because I had been raised as a Southern Baptist, I didn't know any spirit-filled people who spoke in tongues. So I decided to venture out and see who I could connect with who had a faith like mine. As I searched, I went from group to group, encountering some really bizarre things.

I'll never forget one Bible study I attended. I was very excited to be there because a woman was coming who had a reputation for having a special relationship with the Holy Spirit. To my surprise, when she arrived, she came and sat right next to me, and I couldn't wait to see what was going to happen that evening.

As all of us were worshiping God and praying in tongues, suddenly this woman next to me began to say loudly, "*OHHH! Ohhhh!*"

Now, I had never heard anything like that in my Baptist church. With great alarm, I looked at her and asked, "Is something wrong?"

She said, "*Oh! Ohhh! He's here! He's here!*"

"Who's here?" I asked.

"*The Holy Spirit,*" she replied. "*The Holy Spirit is here!*"

Well, that's what my heart was longing to see and experience. So, with great excitement, I looked at her and asked, "Where? Where is the Holy Spirit?"

Pulling back her sleeves, she said, "Do you see these goose bumps on my arms? *That's* the manifestation of the Holy Spirit!"

Immediately, I pulled back my sleeve and saw that I had goosebumps too. But I knew mine were the result of the air conditioning being too low in the house, and I was freezing.

Holy Ghost goosebumps? I thought to myself. *I've never heard of such a thing.* And the more I thought about it, the more it turned me off.

Nevertheless, I continued my search, going from group to group to group. It seemed like the Charismatics I met who spoke in tongues were totally led by feelings. While some searched for goosebumps, others waited for chills to move up and down their spine. If they didn't experience a feeling like this, they felt like the Holy Spirit never showed up — a mindset that continued to turn me off.

Growing up in the Baptist church, we were taught *not* to be led by our emotions. To me, that's what these Charismatics were doing. They ran from meeting to meeting, always trying to get another feeling of goosebumps or shivers up and down their spine.

With a growing frustration, I began to pray, "Lord, I know my experience is real and that I've genuinely been baptized in the Holy Spirit. But Lord, I'm looking for more than a feeling. I don't just want goosebumps; I want You to satisfy the aching in my heart."

The Lord heard my cry.

One day, when I came home from school and turned on the radio, I heard beautiful piano music playing. I didn't know it then, but the person playing was a man named Dino, a highly anointed musician who later became my friend.

The announcer burst in and said, "Here she is — the young lady you've been waiting for — Kathryn Kuhlman."

That was the first time I had heard of Kathryn Kuhlman. If you're younger, you may not know who Kathryn Kuhlman is, but she had one of the greatest miracle ministries in the last century.

"Hello there!" she said with a smile. "Have you been waiting for me? Today, I want to talk to you about the communion of the Holy Spirit."

In that moment, it was like her voice reached through the radio and grabbed hold of me. Indeed, I had been waiting for her, and her ministry in my life was remarkably life-giving.

My experience with Kathryn Kuhlman's teachings is one reason I believe media ministry is so powerful. At a very young age, she impacted me, and I became hooked on her daily radio program.

From that point on, every day at three o'clock in Tulsa, Oklahoma, I would turn on my radio, lean on the kitchen cabinet, and wait for Kathryn Kuhlman to say, "Hello there! Have you been waiting for me?" And every day I would say, "Yes, Kathryn. I'm here waiting for you! Let's get started!"

The day she began speaking about the communion of the Holy Spirit is one I will always remember. It was a subject I had never heard taught. The only time I heard the word "communion" was when our church had the Lord's Supper, which we sometimes called communion.

What is the communion of the Holy Spirit? I thought. It was that day that Kathryn Kuhlman began to describe communion as a divine fellowship with the Spirit of God.

As the Lord would have it, I ended up serving in one of her meetings in Tulsa not too long after that. Because I had heard the choir had the best seats closest to the stage, I joined up. Sure enough, being in the choir gave me a front-row view of all the miracles.

As I took my place and we began to worship and sing "How Great Thou Art," Kathryn came on stage, and for the first time in my life, I saw a human being interfacing with the Holy Spirit. It was one of the most beautiful things I've ever seen in my life.

I watched in amazement as she and the Holy Spirit began to work together on that stage. Under His direction, she began to speak words of knowledge, describing in detail certain ailments people in the audience were experiencing of which she had no previous knowledge. As she did, people began to be healed all over the auditorium.

When I left that meeting, I wanted more. I couldn't shake the longing for a deeper experience in the Spirit. In addition to praying in tongues, I longed to experience and begin living in communion with the Holy Spirit.

Then one day — after searching and searching — I came across a Bible verse that really changed me. It became, and still is, a foundational verse in my life.

The 'Communion of the Holy Spirit'

The scripture that Rick discovered is found in Paul's second letter to the believers at Corinth. As the apostle concluded his message, he said:

> **The grace of the Lord Jesus Christ, and the love of God, and the communion of the Holy [Spirit], be with you all. Amen.**
> **— 2 Corinthians 13:14**

Many believers know about the grace of God because it touched their lives and brought them the gift of salvation. They are also familiar with the love of God, which is inseparable from His saving grace. The Bible says, "…God demonstrates his own love for us in this: While we were still sinners, Christ died for us" (Romans 5:8 *NIV*).

It is the last part of Second Corinthians 13:14 that many Christians struggle to grasp.

What is the communion of the Holy Spirit? And how is it to *be with us all?* To help answer this question, we turn to the original text for the meaning of the word "communion." In Greek, it is the word *koinonia*, which carries the idea of *fellowship, partnership,* and *responsibility.*

What is interesting is that when you search for this word *koinonia* in the New Testament and see how it is used, you can gain very important insight as to what the communion of the Holy Spirit is. For example, consider Paul's words to the believers in Galatia. He said:

> **And when James, Cephas, and John, who seemed to be pillars, perceived the grace that was given unto me, they gave to me and Barnabas the right hands of fellowship….**
> **— Galatians 2:9**

In the original text, the word "fellowship" is the Greek word *koinonia*. Thus, what Paul is saying here is that James, Cephas [Peter], and John gave him and Barnabus the right hand of *koinonia*, which in context here means that these leaders in the Church invited Paul and Barnabas into their inner circle. It was a very tight circle in which few people were invited. But those that were a part of it shared intimate *fellowship* and *partnership.*

That is one of the primary meanings of the communion of the Holy Spirit. It is the Holy Spirit inviting us into His inner circle — a very special place of relationship reserved for His closest friends. Feelings of goosebumps and chills will come and go, but intimacy (*koinonia*) with the Holy Spirit is lasting and fulfilling.

Our Place of Deepest Intimacy With the Holy Spirit Is in Our 'Closet'

Another meaningful example of communion is found in Matthew 6 where Jesus talks about prayer. Before He shares what we have come to know as the Lord's Prayer, He says:

> **But thou, when thou prayest, enter into thy closet, and when thou hast shut thy door, pray to thy Father which is in secret; and thy Father which seeth in secret shall reward thee openly.**
> — **Matthew 6:6**

Take a close look at the word *closet*. Jesus said when you pray, "enter thy closet." In Greek, the word "closet" is *tameion*, which depicts *a secret place where one would hide his most valuable possessions*. This was a secure place like *a safety deposit box*, where your priceless possessions were kept under lock and key. Eventually, this word *tameion* came to describe a place like *a bank* where you could keep your money so it would be safe, and by Early New Testament times, the word "closet" evolved again and came to describe a *bedroom*.

A bedroom is a *secret place* where priceless, treasured things occur between a husband and a wife. When moments of intimacy transpire between a married couple, children are not allowed inside. The couple goes into the bedroom and shuts the door. It is a time of intimacy that is shared only between the two of them. It is deeply private.

By using this word "closet" (*tameion*), Jesus is telling us that we can come to know God in intimate fellowship. But to do that, we need time to get alone with the Holy Spirit for fellowship — a time that belongs only to the Holy Spirit and us personally.

Now praying with others is important and powerful. Husbands and wives should pray together, just as families and churches should pray together. But there needs to be a time set aside when each person spends intimate time alone in prayer — just that person and the Holy Spirit. In that place of intimacy, each of us are to share our heart with the Holy Spirit and listen as He speaks to us. Jesus had times when He fellowshipped with the

Spirit, and no one was there. All through the gospels, we read about Him getting up early and going to the mountains, the desert, or the seaside to pray by Himself.

Some feel the proper daily hour to "commune" with the Holy Spirit is in the early hours of the morning, and that certainly can be a great time to be alone before your day gets underway. But the issue is not the hour; the issue is *isolation*. You can have your time of fellowship with the Holy Spirit in the morning or in the evening. He will meet you on a walk, in the car, or in the shower. The point is not where or when you meet — the point is that you find a time and a place that works best for you to be alone with the Holy Spirit and not be interrupted.

This is a sacred time of divine communion with the Father through the Holy Spirit. It is a sweet mingling together of human spirit with divine Spirit.

Communion With the Spirit Means 'Partnership' With the Spirit

In addition to intimate fellowship, *koinonia* — communion with the Holy Spirit — also includes the idea of *partnership*. We find this demonstrated in Luke 5:7, which says, "And they beckoned unto their *partners*, which were in the other ship, that they should come and help them...." In this passage, Peter and those with him in his boat had so many fish they couldn't handle them alone. So they called out to their "partners" (*koinonia*) in the other boat to come over and help them.

By using the word *koinónia*, Luke meant that the people in the other boat were Peter's legitimate business partners. They were in the fishing business together, and that is what the word *koinónia* also communicates.

Again, this is the same word that is translated as "communion" in Second Corinthians 13:14, which means the Holy Spirit wants to be a legitimate partner in all the business of your life. He wants to work with you, serve with you, help you, and empower you.

Communion With the Spirit
Also Means He Takes 'Responsibility' for Us

One other meaning of the word *koinonia* is the idea of *responsibility*. This is illustrated in the apostle Paul's letter to the Philippians. After these believers had sent Paul a huge offering to help carry on his ministry, he wrote back to them and said:

> **Notwithstanding ye have well done, that ye did communicate with my affliction.**
> **— Philippians 4:14**

The word "communicate" in this verse is the Greek word *koinónia*, and its use here tells us the Philippians didn't just hear about Paul's problems and say, "We'll pray for you, brother." Instead, they took up an offering because they felt *a sense of responsibility* for him, and the money they sent helped him in his affliction.

Keep in mind, the Greek word *koinónia* also carries the idea of *fellowship, intimacy,* and *partnership*. Therefore, in addition to the Holy Spirit wanting *fellowship, intimacy,* and *partnership*, He also has a deep *sense of responsibility* to take care of us.

As we close out this lesson, let's look once more at the amazing words Paul speaks to close his second letter to the Corinthian believers:

> **The grace of the Lord Jesus Christ, and the love of God, and the communion of the Holy [Spirit], be with you all. Amen.**
> **— 2 Corinthians 13:14**

Friend, the *fellowship, intimacy, partnership,* and *responsibility* of the Holy Spirit is to be with ALL of us — not just a few select people or a special group. This intimate communion is for each and every one of us — including *YOU!*

QUESTIONS AND ANSWERS WITH RICK RENNER

In the program, Rick answered the following question from one of our viewers.

Q. Was Jesus rich or was He poor?

A. "I've been asked this question a few times," Rick said. "And the Scripture people will often quote to me is Second Corinthians 8:9, which says:

> **For ye know the grace of our Lord Jesus Christ, that, though he was rich, yet for your sakes he became poor, that ye through his poverty might be rich.**

"Obviously, Jesus was rich in Heaven before He came to earth as a baby. In that sense, we know He left all his heavenly riches behind, and by comparison, became poor. However, as a baby around the age of two, Jesus was showered with gifts brought by the wise men (*see* Matthew 2:1-11). Those gifts provided for Him, Mary, and Joseph while living down in Egypt, and it is believed they also provided funding for Jesus' earthly ministry.

"Jesus never used the riches He was given for selfish purposes. In that sense, He made Himself poor and actually surrendered His life so that we spiritually might become rich."

STUDY QUESTIONS

> **Study to shew thyself approved unto God, a workman that needeth not to be ashamed, rightly dividing the word of truth.**
> **— 2 Timothy 2:15**

1. Does Rick's journey sound familiar? In what ways can you personally relate to the story he shared about seeking to know more about the person of the Holy Spirit?
2. In Matthew 6:6, Jesus said that when you pray, you are to go into your *closet*, shut the door, and pray to your Father in secret. What new insights did you learn from this lesson about the remarkable word "closet" and its connection to experiencing intimacy with God?
3. As believers, intimate fellowship with the Holy Spirit and with one another is a vital part of our existence. What else does the Bible say about healthy fellowship in First Corinthians 1:9; Philippians 2:1-3; and First John 1:1-7? And according to First Corinthians 10:20-22;

Second Corinthians 6:14-18; and Ephesians 5:11, what kind of fellowship are we instructed to *avoid*? Reflect on these passages and listen for what the Holy Spirit reveals to you.

PRACTICAL APPLICATION

But be ye doers of the word, and not hearers only,
deceiving your own selves.
—James 1:22

1. To experience intimate fellowship with the Holy Spirit, we must set aside regular time to meet with Him by ourselves. Have you been able to do that? What time and place works best for you to be alone and spend uninterrupted time with Him? If you want more *alone time* with the Holy Spirit, pray and ask Him what you can remove from your schedule to create space to be with Him.

2. Have you been baptized in the Holy Spirit, and have you received the gift of tongues? If so, how would describe your experience? How has this deeper level of intimacy with the Spirit changed your life? How would you encourage a friend to seek the baptism in the Holy Spirit?

3. If you have not been baptized in the Holy Spirit but would like to be, you can! All you have to do is ask — that's what Jesus Himself says about the Holy Spirit in Luke 11:9-13. Take time to read this passage and get alone with God. Repent of any sin in your life, and ask Him to baptize you in the Holy Spirit.

Notes

_____

_____

_____

_____

_____

_____

_____

_____

_____

_____

_____

_____

_____

_____

_____

_____

_____

_____

_____

_____

_____

_____

_____

_____

_____

_____

_____

_____

_____

_____

CLAIM YOUR FREE RESOURCE!

As a way of introducing you further to the teaching ministry of Rick Renner, we would like to send you FREE of charge his teaching, "How To Receive a Miraculous Touch From God" on CD or as an MP3 download.

In His earthly ministry, Jesus commonly healed *all* who were sick of *all* their diseases. In this profound message, learn about the manifold dimensions of Christ's wisdom, goodness, power, and love toward all humanity who came to Him in faith with their needs.

☑ **YES, I want to receive Rick Renner's monthly teaching letter!**

Simply scan the QR code to claim this resource or go to: **renner.org/claim-your-free-offer**

WITH US!

renner.org

www.ingramcontent.com/pod-product-compliance
Lightning Source LLC
Chambersburg PA
CBHW071644040426
42452CB00009B/1762